WALKING IN GOD'S PURPOSE

PASTOR REBECCA SULLIVAN

It is our prayer and declaration that you would maintain a Spirit of Integrity concerning the knowledge shared with you in this book. Meaning when using the information in this book publicly, you would give the Author Pastor Rebecca Sullivan proper recognition and acknowledgement for the knowledge, work, experience, research, and labor of development of this book.

No part of this book may be reproduced by mimeograph process or by another method of duplication unless expressed written permission has been granted by Pastor Rebecca Sullivan.

Thank You In Advance
for you countenance of righteousness and obedience.

Ecclesiastes 12:14

For God shall bring every work into judgment, with every secret thing, whether it be good or whether it be evil.

First Edition: 2021
ISBN: 978-1-934905-11-1

Worldwide Kingdom Publishing
1911 Horger St
Lincoln Park, Michigan 48146

Copyright 2021 by Pastor Rebecca Sullivan
All rights reserved.

PREFACE

In today's society, so many people do not understand their purpose. They do not realize God has a purpose for their life. Once you are born, purpose begins and it is our responsibility to discover what our purpose is, in this world. The way you can discover your purpose in life is to read the word of God, building a prayer life, and by understanding your gifts and talents. Also, another method of discovering your purpose is by receiving counsel and prophetic confirmations through dreams and visions: which will show you what God created you to do in life.

In order to understand purpose we must examine the definition. According to the internet dictionary, **purpose** is the reason why someone and something exists, or it reveals how a thing is done, made, used, and created. Therefore, our purpose in God is the reason why He created us and His intentions for us in the earth.

In conclusion, there is no excuse why we should not know our purpose in life. We have to search and seek God for His purpose in our life. Our purpose is not what we think it should be; but it is what God ordained it to be. In reading this book, and the information provided for you; you will discover your purpose and be encouraged to walk in God's purpose for your life!

DEDICATION

This is dedicated to my mother the late, Emma Johnson; my sister, the late Patricia Johnson-Walker; to my aunts the late, Aunt Jessie Kuykendall and the late, Aunt Deola Mitchell.

This book is dedicated to men and women who are waiting on the promise to be married. Marriage is honorable in the sight of God. Therefore, it is purposed for you to be married, this will encourage you to wait on the Lord for the mate He has for you. Know assuredly, you must be still to hear the voice of the Lord when He speaks to you. He may be the person next to you; and you are not aware of the blessing!

This book is also dedicated to the people who may be single, widowed, and divorced; but yet, desire companionship and to be married. I want to encourage you to ask God for the mate you desire; we have not because we ask not! God is concerned about everything that concerns you.

Isaiah 40:31

But they that wait upon the Lord shall renew their strength; they shall mount up with wings as eagles; they shall run, and not be weary; and they shall walk, and not faint.

SPECIAL THANKS

Special thanks to, my Lord & Savior Jesus Christ who empowered me to write this book!

Special thanks to, my husband, Assistant Pastor Darwin L. Sullivan you are a great encourager and supporter of this project! Thank you, Sweetie, you are the Love of my life!

Special thanks to, Apostle Charissee Lewis and Pastor Rudy M. Lewis, Jr. for assisting me and bringing out the writer in me!

Special thanks to, Bishop Roderic A. Edwards & Rachel Edwards.

Special thanks to, Bishop Shedrick Clark & Dr. Sandra Clark.

Special thanks to, Bishop Russell Schaller.

Special thanks to, Pastor Larry Robinson & Lady Teresa Robinson.

Special thanks to, Prophetess Ebony Etheridge for encouraging me to write this book.

Special thanks to, Eugena Johnson, Barbara Campbell, Kenyona Archibald, Kimberley Galard, Valerie D. Perkins, Tamiko Jones.

Special thanks to, Apostle Gwen Hudson thank you for your encouragement and support. Thank you for directing my wedding.

INTRODUCTION

Have you ever felt like there was more in life for you; but you could not pin point what it was? Have you felt like something was missing in your life? Have you ever felt like you was just existing with no purpose? As a child, being raised in Church, attending Sunday school, and bible class faithfully; but yet, I did not know my purpose in life. The lack of not knowing my God ordained purpose, caused me to have low self-esteem. I felt that I could not accomplish anything and that I could not do anything right. It had a negative affect on my outlook of life. It was so detrimental that when people called me names; such as "you're black" it made me cry. The name calling cause me to want to be, white; because it seemed to me that the white people had the best of everything. They had good schools, great colleges, good jobs that paid more money; this mindset caused me to be very angry. By being angry, it affected me in school, in relationships, and my ability to understand new concepts. I had a difficult time comprehending and learning. It affected my grades; reading and writing became my worst enemy. I missed a lot of opportunities, because of my reading and writing. I could not get the best jobs: for example, I went to several colleges and I received my bachelor's and master's degree in business administration. My second master's in education; but I struggled to get through to complete my classes. Even though I had all of these degrees I did not work in the field of my career. I did not receive the money for all the degrees that I had earned. I did my student teaching from a mentor who I thought would guide me and be a great model for me; unfortunately, she spoke a lot of negativity in my life. She tried to fail me from receiving my master's degree and teaching education; but God stepped in and my supervisor overrode her decisions, and I received my Master's Degree. After I received my Master's Degree and I had to take the test. I failed the tests many times and I had to resort to being a substitute teacher. I cried many nights from not passing the test which hinder me from being a teacher. This also was a reason why I dealt with low self-esteem.

Lastly, when working at different jobs as a substitute teacher for over 15 years I had some good and bad experiences. Sometimes the teachers I substituted for, would speak negative comments about my style of teaching and this would hinder me from coming back to the school. They said I did not follow the lesson plans the way they wanted me to. The kids would say I was mean to them; because I did not tolerate belligerent behavior in the class, such as cussing, fighting, and defiant attitudes. However the positive side of this, is that I had children who respected me and called me their "Grandmother", the Whites, Mexicans, and Blacks children. I can remember having a bad experience while teaching a 6th grade class for 5 months. The students would say they enjoyed me, but when the teacher came back she accused me of stealing candy and money out of her drawers. She asked them and they told her the students who took it; but she falsely accused me and the principal banned me from the school, because he believed her lies. They tried to make me loose my license as a substitute teacher, but my employer intervene and did not allow it to happen.

In conclusion, I realized it was time for me to retire from substitute teaching when a 5th grade boy accused me of hitting him. His parents came up to the school and they came into my classroom. I was oblivious to the situation and I was called in the office and approached about what the 5th grade boy accused me of and they began to tell me about Michigan laws and policies concerning this manner. They proceeded to investigate the situation and discovered I was not working that day. It was at that moment, I said *"Enough is Enough"* knowing this part of my life was over. Needless to say I was very upset, angry, and I cried, because of the mistreatment, once again. Again, God divine intervention vindicated me from the attack of the enemy! I give Him all the Glory! He is so faithful about processing us into our purpose!

Psalms 138:8

The LORD will perfect *that which* **concerneth me: thy mercy O LORD,** *endureth* **for ever: forsake not the works of thine own hands.**

Note to the Readers

Reader, be encouraged to know that God is right here to meet your needs and your desire for a significant other. Because God loves you and wants the best for you; you must know that He will never leave you; nor forsaken you. Trust in the Lord with all thy heart and lean not unto thy own understanding and in all thy ways acknowledge Him and He shall direct thy path, **Proverbs 3:5-6.**

Reader, while you are waiting for your mate you must activate your faith. Activating your faith is believing God for your promise. Therefore, step out on faith and find a dress, look at rings, and plan your wedding. These are actions that indicate that you are trusting God for your mate.

Reader, remember to wait on the Lord and be of a good cheer, because your companion is on the way! As you follow your process and walk in God's Purpose; you will not be lead wrong;

but this time next year you will have your mate!

TABLE OF CONTENTS

Preface
Dedication
Special Thanks
Introduction
Note to Reader

PART ONE: EARLY YEARS

Chapter One: TRAIN UP A CHILD

Chapter Two: FINDING MYSELF

Chapter Three: PLEASING PEOPLE

PART TWO: UNDERSTANDING GOD'S PURPOSE

Chapter Four: UNDERSTANDING GOD'S PURPOSE

Chapter Five: BIBLICAL EXAMPLES of WALKING GOD'S PURPOSE

PART THREE: UNDERSTANDING FAITH

Chapter Six: BUILDING UP YOUR FAITH

Chapter Seven: RECEIVING THE PROMISE

PART ONE

THE EARLY YEARS

CHAPTER ONE

TRAIN UP A CHILD

Scripture: Proverbs 22:6
Train up a child in the way he should go: and when he is old, he will not depart from it.

Do you remember a time when it took a village to raise a child? The parents supported community discipline: the neighbors, schools, and churches collaborated in the raising children. Do you remember a time when children were taught to say "yes ma'am, and yes sir to their elders out of respect?" The manners that were taught in my days in the 50's, 60's, and 70's are obsolete. There is no more "yes ma'am and yes sir", no more community discipline, and no more church, and school support; because some of the parents of today slander your name, threaten, and fight anyone who tries to correct their children. Then when the child gets in trouble, put in prison, or even killed; then they cry, "Where is the support, and where is God?" Then you blame everybody else; but yourself!

As parents, church leaders, educators, and caregivers we have a responsibility to train up our children in the fear and admiration of the Lord. This means spending quality time as a family, praying, reading your word, going to church, eating meals together, and having consistent communication with children to understand their issues. Instead of parents being in their separate rooms, and the children on the computers, and playing video games. Parents should spend at least two hours a day with your children to teach and train them in the way they should go, according to the word of God.

As adults, we should live by examples and demonstrating God's love in the life that we live. We can not live a raggedy lifestyle and expect our children to obey and respect us. They should see us going to church, praying, attending Sunday school, and Bible class. This is an intricate part of us training the child in the ways of God and teaching them responsibility, respect, and treating others righteously. Knowing that, when we treat people right; right will come back to us; but if we treat people wrong, then wrong will also come back to us. The bible tells, according to Galatians:

Galatians 6:7
Be not deceived; God is not mocked: for whatsoever a man soweth, that shall he also reap.

In examining this scripture, there are four words we shall define: **deceived, mocked, soweth, and reap.** According to Merriam-Webster Dictionary, *deceived* is defined as to cause to accept as true or valid that which is false or invalid. *Mocked* is defined as being treated with contempt or ridicule, it disappoints the hopes of a person. Next, is *soweth* means to plant seed for growth especially by scattering and to set something in motion. Lastly, the word *reap* mean to gather a harvest and to win. When children follow these guidelines they will know how to cope with problems, issues, or concerns in a healthy manner; in stead of turning to drugs, alcohol, and sexual encounters. Most importantly, they can go to God for themselves to receive the help they need.

When I was growing up, my sister and I was raised by parents who valued traditions. When we were raised during a time where the neighbors were an intricate part of our discipline. We were not allowed to talk back to our elders, or adults. We were taught to respect them at all times, whether we agreed with them or not. Our parents made sure we spent quality time as a family: by going to church, a family outing, movie theater, riding around Belle Isle, the State Fair, the Thanksgiving Day Parade, Big Boy restaurant, and the Flaming Emeralds restaurant. They taught us how to pray, as a family. They taught how to cook and clean to keep the household in order. We also had chores which made us responsible. When our parents had a disagreement; we were not present. They did not allow us to see or hear their arguments, therefore, we maintain respect for both of them. As children, we were not allowed to ask one parent; then go to the other parent to get the answer we wanted. This kind of behavior is divisive, manipulative, and crafty. Unfortunately, we are seeing it more and more in children of today. My sister and I were not allowed to fight one another. We had a responsibility to stick together and protect one another, and when we did try to fight: we received a beating of our lives!

In summary, I want to reiterate we as adults and parents have a great responsibility to teach our children the value of bringing out the hidden gifts and talents that are dormant within them. It is our responsibility to teach them their purpose in God and their purpose in life. It is sad to say, so many children do not know who they are and what they are; therefore, they can not reach their full potential. They should be able to express themselves, whether good, bad or indifferent. It is important so they can cope with their issues and receive the help they need. When children bottle up their feelings that is when the enemy attacks their mind with thoughts of suicide, low self-esteem, rejection, and loneliness. We must continue to train up our children and speak positive words, and words of affirmations to our children. When parents speak negativity to their children; it could damage their ability to succeed in anything. The negative words from a parent can sometimes make a child feel he or she is not good enough; and this can affect them for the rest of their lives. The parents have an important role in the development and growth of their children. The parents are models and examples to the children; because children are always watching the behavior of their parents to see how they cope with life. This is crucial because it teaches the children how to live with proper morals and values; which causes the child to grow up as a respectful adult. This is essential, because they can teach and impart to their children the same values of what they were raised by. Even in today's society, we must continue to train our children in the way they should go, by looking at positive examples of their parental legacy, prayer, and the Word of God!

CHAPTER TWO

FINDING MYSELF

As a young adult, did you know where you were going in life? As a young adult, did you know your purpose in the world? As a young adult, did you have an identity crisis? Many times, when young people reach the age of adulthood; they refuse to listen and they think they know everything. A lot of young adults make unnecessary mistakes, because they refuse to listen to the voice of wisdom from their parents, elders, teachers, even friends who they associate with. They find themselves dealing with many situations that are difficult to get out of; such as, drugs, pregnancy, alcohol addictions, smoking weed, and still they do not know who they are. They do not realize after they finish the rebellious behavior; they are in the same situations, because they feel they are grown. Many young adults quit before they start their process of life; by dropping out of school, grades not being adequate to get them in the best colleges, or being introduced to credit cards and accumulating debt. They are not educated on the value of starting your own business, and while in high school missing out on the opportunities of skills and careers trades.

As a young adult, I had the opportunity of being in school, trying to find myself, but due to lack of understanding I was not able to get into the prestigious schools. I did not receive the help that I needed to prepare me for college. Therefore, by not seeking the proper counsel for college, I went to college and receive many degrees my Associate, Bachelor's in Business Administration, and two Master's Degree; one in Business Administration and the other in Educational Teaching. Unfortunately, I have not worked in the career fields and I have never received the pay of my value; because the opportunity was not there for me to work. As young adults, we have to realize we must search for the information we need for our lives; because, people will not openly share what they know. There is no reason a young person in this society can not find what they want to do, we are living in an informational age; where knowledge is at your fingertips. You can google, research, read, and also, you can talk to people in your career interest, who does not mind sharing knowledge of their profession. There are many ways you can receive what you need to learn about advancing your life. The young people of today must be aggressive, and not lazy in order to discover what they need to build a successful life. It is important that you surround yourself with positive young people who understand the value of being positive go-getters in life. They are not distracted by partying and negative activities and negative people that will effect their minds to bring them down. Because what comes out of your mouth reveals who you really are; for instance, if you say I can't do this, you will not do it. But if you say, I can do all things through Christ which strengtheneth me, Philippians 4:13; you will achieve it. In preparing yourself as a young adult, these are some of the things you can get to find yourself; career choices, information on business and finance, preparation for marriage, knowledge on being celibate as a single adult, and how to save money.

In closing, it was difficult for me to find myself because of low self-esteem, negative thoughts, and feeling of inadequacy of reaching my goals, at that time. I had the training; but I was not able to receive wise counsel in the career of my choice. One thing we must realize, we can not blame others for not achieving what we want. We must take responsibility for our own lives. No one can hinder you of what you want to do; but you can hinder yourself by not seeking the knowledge you need to advance. You can not be afraid of receiving "No" or fear the rejection of others when it comes to your career. You must keep pursuing your dreams, your visions, and your goals of what you want to do in life. Life is not going to come to you; you must be active and pursue your purpose. There is no reason a young person should be ignorant; our young people should refrain from video games, and social media and choose to do something productive with their lives. Sometimes, you must be alone and not be in the company of friends; so God can talk to you one on one, and give you the direction you need about your own life.

CHAPTER THREE

PLEASING PEOPLE

Have you found yourself trying to be accepted by other people because you want to make them happy? Have you found yourself trying to please people, when they only want your full attention to focus on them and not others? Have you found yourself pleasing people by agreeing with everything they say and do, because you fear confrontations? The definition of a people pleaser is a person who has an emotional need to please others and at the expense of his or her needs or desires, according to Merriam Webster Dictionary. In everyday living in this society, a person can lose their true identity in trying to please others just to keep their friendship. There are many people who are bound, hindered, and confused; because they are trying to be accepted by others. People pleasers most of the time, get their feelings hurt and are abused; because they go out of their way to make others happy while not being happy themselves. It is sad, when you find a person that is selfish and they always want you to give them; but when you need help they are no where to be found. It is a known fact, that people pleasers suffer from depression, and rejection; sometimes making themselves sick, when they can not get the attention of a certain person. People pleasers sometimes feel unloved and alone, because they are not reciprocated the love they give to others.

Deuteronomy 31:8
And the LORD, he it is that doth go before thee; he will be with thee, he will not fail thee, neither forsake thee: fear not, neither be dismayed.

Psalm 55:22
Cast thy burden upon the LORD, and he shall sustain thee: he shall never suffer the righteous to be moved.

When I was dealing with people pleasers, there were people in my life who tried to control my friendships. They did not want me to be friends with certain people, they would get mad at me for correcting them. They wanted me to please them. Being a people pleaser will cause you to miss out on your own purpose by trying to please others. Controlling people will stop talking to you when you refuse to do what they want you to do, because they want to manipulate you and make you please them. It is important to identify the characteristics of a people pleaser. On the next page, we share 10 signs of a people pleaser.

There are **10 signs** to identify if you are a people pleaser according to **Psychology Today: www.psychologytoday.com**

1) **You pretend to agree with everyone.**

2) **You feel responsible for how other people feel.**

3) You apologize often.

4) You feel burdened by the things you have to do.

5) You can't say no.

6) You feel uncomfortable if someone is angry at you.

7) You act like the people around you.

8) You need praises to feel good.

9) You go to great lengths to avoid conflict.

10) You don't admit when your feelings are hurt.

In closing, you must be yourself and not allow people to manipulate you into doing, saying, and being someone God has not called you to be. You must remember God's purpose in your life by not getting off focus and becoming a people pleaser. God made us all different therefore, you must have a made up mind to believe God and not people. Most of the time, people pleasers do not trust God they are trusting someone else for their happiness. The people pleasers cannot stand on their own. The Word of God tells us according to Proverbs,

Proverbs 3:5-6
Trust in the Lord with all thine heart; and lean not unto thine own understanding. In all thy ways acknowledge him, and he shall direct thy paths.

In addition to, people pleasing sometimes is rooted in low self-esteem. They feel they can not accomplish anything without the approval of others. They seek validation and praises of others to make them feel important. People pleaser need to remove the masks they wear, because they conceal their true feelings for fear of rejection. It is my prayer, that you are not a people pleaser and that you trust God in every area of your life. Remember you are unique, because God made you that way!

PART TWO

UNDERSTANDING GOD'S PURPOSE

CHAPTER FOUR

UNDERSTANDING GOD'S PURPOSE

Do you know anyone who doesn't know their purpose? Do you know anyone that have not discovered God's purpose until they are mature in age? It's sad to say, so many people have died; and yet, have not understood God's purpose in their life. Everyone born needs to understand God's purpose for their life. When you consider the word "***purpose***" according to **https://www.merriam-webster.com** it means the reason something is done or used: the aim or intention of something: the feeling of being determined to do or achieve something: the aim or goal of a person: what a person is trying to do. Therefore, when we look at ***God's Purpose*** for a person's life; it means we must examine scriptures according to the book of Ephesians,

Ephesians 1:4-5

According as he hath chosen us in him before the foundation of the world, that we should be holy and without blame before him in love: Having predestinated us unto the adoption of children by Jesus Christ to himself, according to the good pleasure of his will,

Even before the foundations of the world, God has a divine purpose for our lives. It is His will that we follow the blueprint He has for our lives; be it, schooling, career, marriage, family, business, and ministry. So many people in this society miss the purpose of God; because they do not know how to seek God for the purpose He has for their lives. As a result, they walk in their own understanding which is contrary to God's will. It is essential that we walk in the purpose of God. So we are not persuaded to allow self or others to cause us to miss our purpose in God.

In order to discover your life's purpose in God, you should be guided by the following procedures below:

1) Build a personal relationship with God.

2) Praying.

3) Have a listening ear to the voice of God.

4) Study and mediate on God's word.

5) Read materials of others who walked in God's purpose.

6) Listen and obey your Spiritual Leaders who have your best interest at heart.

7) Walk by faith by trusting God.

8) Become a doer, not just hearer only.

9) Take the limits off of God.

10) Eradicate fear.

In conclusion, you can see God love us and He wants what's best for us in every area of our lives. We must deny our own self-will and give up what we want to do to fulfill God's purpose.

Many people may not agree with the way God's is taking us to fulfill the purpose of God in our lives. When we fulfill God's purpose we will have so much joy and peace in our lives; knowing, that we are being about our Father's business! Do not accept any negative vibes from within that would make you doubt and become discouraged. The enemy's job is to stop you from fulfilling your destiny. The bible declares according to John 10,

John 10:10
The thief cometh not, but for to steal, and to kill, and to destroy: I am come that they might have life, and that they might have it more abundantly.

It is imperative for us to surround ourselves with positive people who will encourage us to walk in God's purpose. We do not need anyone in our lives who are jealous, negative, and fearful. The people who operate with these evil spirits can do damage and destroy your whole purpose in God, if you let them control your mind. So remember, God is on your side. He will never leave you; therefore, go forth, be strong, and courageous in your endeavors to please God by walking in your divine purpose.

CHAPTER FIVE

BIBLICAL EXAMPLES OF WALKING IN GOD'S PURPOSE

Do you know anyone in the Bible who walked in God's purpose victoriously? Are you familiar with any characters in the Bible who achieved their purpose in God? Do you know prophets who remind you of yourself in walking in God's purpose? In the previous chapter, we shared with you the definition of ***purpose***: <u>the aim or goal of a person: what a person is trying to do</u>. There is no one in this world that is born; that God does not have a purpose for; He has a plan the moment we were created. His plan for us is to discover our purpose through the Holy Ghost. We all have responsibilities to walk in our own purpose, no matter if others may think or feel differently. It is all about us being obedient to do what God tells us to do. The bible tells us in the book of Isaiah,

Isaiah 54:17

No weapon that is formed against thee shall prosper; and every tongue that shall rise against thee in judgment thous shalt condemn. This is the heritage of the servants of the Lord, and their righteousness is of me, saith the Lord.

Satan will use people to discourage you from pleasing God, and walking in your purpose. He will use people who do not believe like you, to put a damper on your abilities to go forth. He does this by inciting jealousy, envy, and strife in the hearts of others; so they can not see the purpose God has for them. When walking in God's purpose we can not be ignorant of satan's devices, lest he will get an advantage of us.

II Corinthians 2:11

Lest satan should get an advantage of us: for we are not ignorant of his devices.

There are times when walking in God's purpose you may be confronted by mockery, ridicule, and criticism, because people do not want you to grow further than where they can grow. They are intimidated and do not want you to surpass them in purpose. When we discuss the different characters you will discover what they experienced while walking in God's purpose.

Biblical Examples of Walking in God's Purpose

1} Jesus Christ   7}Deborah
2} Noah   8} Anna
3} Abraham   9} Mary
4} Moses   10} Paul
5} Naomi   11} Timothy
6} Daniel   12} Ruth

1} Jesus Christ

Jesus Christ died on the cross for our sins. According to **Isaiah 53:5,** *But he was wounded for our transgressions, he was* *bruised for our iniquities: the chastisement of our peace was upon him; and with his stripes we are healed.*

His purpose was to save us from our sins. Before He was born, Herod tried to kill Him to stop His purpose. In the Garden of Gethsemane, Jesus asked God to let this cup pass from Him: nevertheless not as I will, but as thou wilt, **Matthew 26:39**. During the crucifixion, He was beaten, abused, spit on, and humiliated for the sake of humanity. Jesus went about healing the sick, raising the dead, and feeding the poor. Jesus Christ fulfilled His purpose.

2} Noah

Noah's purpose was to build the ark. According to **Genesis 6:14**, *Make thee an ark of gopher wood; rooms shalt thou make In the ark, and shalt pitch it within and without with pitch.*

God gave him specific instructions on how to do it. He shared with the people that it was going to rain and they mocked him; because it had never rained before in the earth. After Noah completed his assignment, it rained 40 days and 40 nights and God only saved seven members of his family; and he put the animals in the ark two by two. Unfortunately, all those people who mocked him died in the flood.

3} Abraham

Abraham purpose was to be the father of many nations. According to **Genesis 17:4**, *As for me, behold my covenant is with thee, and thou shalt be a father of many nations.* God changed his name from Abram to Abraham and God made a covenant to make him very fruitful. Also, God promised Abraham at the age of hundred years old, and his wife, Sarah at the age of ninety years, that they would have a son. According to, **Genesis 17:16,** *And I will bless her, and give thee a son also of her: yea, I will bless her, and she shall be a mother of nations; kings of* *people shall be of her.* Abraham was a faithful, obedient, man and he walked in his purpose in the Kingdom of God.

4} Moses

Moses purpose was to deliver the children of Israel from Egypt. Before, he reached his purpose: Pharaoh made a decree to kill all male babies. In order to save Moses life, his mother and sister put him in a basket; and the King's daughter found him and he was nursed by his own mother, who was a servant of the King's daughter. When God called Moses and commissioned Moses for his divine purpose in the book of Exodus, he had a supernatural experience with God. In **Exodus 3:5**, *"And he said, Draw not nigh hither: put off thy shoes from off thy feet, for the place whereon thou standest is holy ground."* Before Moses could fulfill the purpose, he had to go through a process of spiritual tests by God. The purpose was finally fulfilled when God harden Pharaoh's heart, the plagues came, and Pharaoh loss his son, according to **Exodus 11:5**.

5} Naomi

Naomi was a godly wife, mother, and mother-in-law. Naomi and her family left Canaan because of a famine, and they moved to the country Moab. They lived there 10 years when her husband and two sons died, and she was left with their two wives. She decided to go back to Bethlehem, and she encouraged her two daughter-in-laws to return to their mother's house. But Ruth did not leave Naomi, she was determined to go with her, **Ruth 1:16-18**. Naomi purpose was to get

Ruth in position to meet Boaz. She also advised Ruth on how to get Boaz attention. *"Wash thyself therefore, and anoint thee, and put thy raiment upon thee, and get thee down to the floor: but make not thyself known unto the man, until he shall have done eating and drinking,* **Ruth 3:3.**

6} Daniel

Daniel purpose was to stand, not compromise his belief, and not defile himself with the portion of the king's meat and wine. Daniel and 2 others were tested for 10 days, they ate vegetables and drank water; while the others ate the royal food and drank wine. In Daniel 1:15-17, *And at the end of ten days their countenances appeared fairer and fatter in the flesh than all the children which did eat the portion of the king's meat. Thus Melzar took away the portion of their meat, and the wine that they should drink; and gave them pulse. As for these four young men,* **God gave them knowledge and skill in all learning and wisdom: and Daniel had understanding in all visions and dreams.** If you want to know more about Daniel's life experiences read the book of Daniel, he prayed 3 times a day, he was put in The Fiery Furnace, and he was taken to the Lion's Den and God brought him through victoriously.

7} Deborah

Deborah was a woman who was a prophetess, the wife of Lapidoth, a strategist, and a judge. She sat under the palm tree and the children of Israel came up to her for judgment. She prophesied to Barak victory over at the Canaanities, Judges 4. In Judges 5, she and Barak sang the song of Deborah to praise the Lord for victory. Deborah purpose was to protect Israel, she was a mother to the people of Israel. **Judges 5:7,** *The inhabitants of the villages ceased, they ceased in Israel, until that I Deborah arose, that I arose a mother in Israel.*

8} Anna

Anna was a prophetess, who came from the tribe of Aser; and she was a wife who married her husband from virginity. She was an intercessor and widow of 84 years old who never left the temple. She served God with fasting and praying night and day. The bible says in **Luke 2:38,** *And she coming in that instant gave thanks* *likewise unto the Lord, and spake of him to all them that looked for redemption in Jerusalem.* So Anna's purpose was to serve God in the temple day and night.

9} Mary

Mary's purpose was to birth Jesus Christ. She was married to Joseph but before they came together, she was found with a child of the Holy Ghost, **Matthew 1:18**. The bible said she shall bring forth a son, and thou shalt call his name JESUS: for he shall save His people from their sin, **Matthew 1:21**. The bible also says, Behold, a virgin shall be with child, and shall bring forth a son, and they shall call his name Emmanuel, which being interpreted is, God with us, **Matthew 1:23**.

10} Paul

Paul, a servant of Jesus Christ, called

to be an Apostle, separated unto the gospel of God, **Romans 1:1**. Paul was once Saul and he had a supernatural encounter with God on the road to Damascus. The bible says in **Acts 9:3-5**, And as he journeyed, he came near Damascus: and suddenly there shined round about him a light from heaven: And he fell to the earth, and heard a voice saying unto him, Saul, Saul, why persecutest thou me? In **Acts 9:15-16**, God reveals Paul's purpose, But the Lord said unto him, Go thy way: for he is a chosen vessel unto me, to bear my name before the Gentiles, and kings, and the children of Israel: For I will shew him how great things he must suffer for my name's sake.

11} Timothy

Timothy's purpose was to preach and

teach the truth, and exposing false doctrines. According to **I Timothy 1:1-2**, Paul, an apostle of Jesus Christ by the commandment of God our Saviour, and Lord Jesus Christ, which is our hope; Unto Timothy, my own son in the faith: Grace, mercy, and peace, from God our Father and Jesus Christ our Lord. Timothy was a young pastor who served God obediently and has two books in the Bible, I Timothy & II Timothy. Timothy received his charge from Apostle Paul according to **I Timothy 1:18-19**, This charge I commit unto thee, son Timothy, according to the prophecies which went before on thee, that thou by them mightest war a good warfare; Holding faith, and a good conscience; which some having put away concerning faith have made shipwreck. Even though Timothy was a young Pastor, he walked in his divine calling.

12} Ruth

Ruth was determined, after her husband died not to return to her mother's homeland; followed Naomi. In **Ruth 1:16,** and Ruth said, Intreat me to not leave thee, or to return from following after thee: for whither thou goest, I will go; and where thou lodgest, I will lodge: thy people shall be my people, and thy God my God. Also, Ruth displayed loyalty and obedience by serving Naomi and following her instructions on receiving her Boaz. The bible reveals this according to **Ruth 4:13-14**, *So Boaz took Ruth, and she was his wife: and when he went* in unto her, the Lord gave her conception and she bare a son. *And the women said unto Naomi, Blessed be the Lord, which hath not left thee this day without a kinsman, that his name May be famous in Israel.* Ruth is know amongst the women of the bible, because she was faithful, obedient, and a virtuous woman. God blessed her with her husband Boaz and she has the book of Ruth in the bible.

PART THREE

UNDERSTANDING FAITH

CHAPTER SIX

BUILDING UP YOUR FAITH

Do you know the meaning of faith? Do you know what it takes to build up your faith? Do you know what the Bible says about faith?

Have you experience anything in your life that required your faith to be strong? The bible has many scriptures concerning faith. Faith, according to <u>Oxford Language Dictionary</u> is complete trust or confidence in someone or something. It also says faith is a strong belief in God or in the doctrines of a religion, based on the spiritual apprehension rather than proof. The bible tells us according to Hebrews,

Hebrews 11:1

Now faith is the substance of things hoped for, and the evidence of things not seen.

II Corinthians 5:9

We walk by faith and not by sight.

In order to build up your faith, you must pray and read your word and become a doer of the Word of God. From experiences in your life, and in your trials and situations that arises it is necessary to believe God and activate your faith. By activating your faith, it will lift up a standard against the enemy that is attacking you. The bible tells us according to Romans,

Romans 10:17

So then faith cometh by hearing, and hearing by the word of God.

It is important for your Christian walk with God to build up your faith by knowing the scriptures, especially when you are believing God for a home, car, spouse, financial increase, your spiritual life, and your purpose. You have to ignore many people who try to discourage you from your faith and walking with God. Many attacks comes from fear and unbelief. The enemy tries to whisper in your ears seeds of doubt but we must understand; when God speaks that settles it and the rest is a done deal. Through dreams and visions, God will show you by faith the solutions to your problems. There are three major words that deal with faith:

    1} Hear - Hear God's word
    2} Trust - Trust God's word
    3} Act - Act upon God's word

When we really hear the voice of God, no stumbling block can get in our way. No matter what it looks like or seem like we know God is able to perform it by faith. Our situation may look unpromising as if the promise is not going to come to pass; but regardless of how it looks God will always bring us through by our faith. I experienced unbelief concerning the timing when God would bless me with a companion. I was in my 60's when God released the promise, my mate. At the age of 64, I had never been married I walked down the aisle with my husband, Darwin Larry Sullivan. Not only that, but God had kept me as a virgin when I received my promise. By faith, I did not have to seek him out, he found me. By faith, one of his daughter Alicia Sullivan-Moore spoke into my life, saying *"God was going to bless me with a husband with an already made family."* We did not realize my husband would be her father; because within the 5 years his wife died, and after that he was seeking for a wife. He came to Goodwill Community Chapel and I met him. I was introduced to him by two young people Michelle and Monica who were joking around and did not realize that he was my true husband, the promise that God sent me. My friend, Barbara Campbell and my mother the late Emma Lee Johnson told me, *"My husband was in the house!"* By faith my mother, my sister, and my two aunties prayed that I would get married before they died, and God answered their prayer. My mom and sister died in 2017, and one aunt died in 2018, and the other aunt died in 2019. They were all at my wedding December 10, 2016. This was truly a faith walk for me. It changed my whole life. Now my faith is stronger than ever before. By faith, I am doing things I never thought I would do, like writing this book and I have my own business paparazziaccessories.com/315919! We are Assistant Pastors of Greater St. John under the leadership of Bishop Russell Schaller. A lot of the members of Goodwill Community Chapel told me not to wait until 2017, but they saw a December wedding for 2016, and by faith I was married. By faith, my director Apostle Gwendolyn Hudson and husband, Pastor Andrew Hudson, and her assistant Gena Johnson sowed into my life; along with my bride maids, sister, members of Goodwill Community Chapel and members of Powerhouse Temple they all made this event one of the most glorious days of my life.

Here are some faith scriptures to assist you in building up your faith.

1} **But without faith it is impossible to please him: for he that cometh to God must believe that he is, and that he is a rewarder of them that diligently seek him. Hebrews 11:6**

2} **And Jesus said unto them, Because of your unbelief: for verily I say unto you, If ye have faith as a grain of mustard seed, ye shall say unto this mountain, Remove hence to yonder place; and** it shall be remove; and nothing shall be impossible unto you. St. Matthew 17:20

3} Jesus answered and said unto them, Verily I say unto you, If ye have faith, and doubt not, ye shall not only do this which is done to the fig tree, but also if ye shall say unto this mountain, be thou removed, and be thou cast into the sea; it shall be done and all things, whatsoever ye shall ask in prayer, believing, ye shall receive. St. Matthew 21:21-22

4} That your faith should not stand in the wisdom of men, but in the power of God. I Corinthians 2:5

5} And he that doubted is damned if he eat, because he eateth not of Faith: for whatsoever is not of faith is sin. Romans 14:23

CHAPTER SEVEN

RECEIVING THE PROMISE

Have you ever been waiting on God to receive your promise? Do you know if God spoke it; it will manifest? Do you know being delayed does not mean you are being denied? The bible tells us in the book of Haggai,

Haggai 2:9
The glory of this latter house shall be greater than of the former saith the Lord of hosts: and in this place will I give peace, saith the Lord of hosts.

A lot people feel that their promise is going to come immediately, and when it does not come fast enough they feel they have not heard from God or they deal with a lack of faith. Sometimes we miss our promise, because we listen to other people and what they think. Instead of believing God, we believe the other person, and forfeit our blessings. Unfortunately, acquaintances, friends, and family members do not see the path and vision God is taking you; and that is when jealousy rises within loves ones and interfere with your receiving your promise. It is not easy when waiting on the promise because you have to constantly prepare yourself for the promise by reading the word, praying, fasting, being obedient to leadership, and being a servant in the house of God.

Hebrews 11:6

But without faith it is impossible to please him: for he that cometh to God must believe that he is, and that he is a rewarder of them that diligently seek him.

Psalm 27:14

Wait on the Lord: be of good courage, and he shall strengthen thine heart: wait, I say, on the Lord.

Matthew 17:20

And Jesus said unto them, Because of your unbelief: for verily I say unto you, If ye have faith as a grain of mustard seed, ye shall say unto this mountain, Remove hence to yonder place; and it shall remove; and nothing shall be impossible unto you.

The scriptures mentioned above will encourage you to wait on your destiny. The number one key is praying, believing God, and hearing his voice. The second key is trusting, and knowing God will do it. The third key is do not listen to anyone that is going to bring doubt to what God has spoken to you.

I am a prime example of many different areas of my life of waiting on God's promises that has come to past.

List of Examples:

1} Never been married and got married on December 10, 2016 at the age of 64 years old.

2} Being diligent about starting my own business August 2, 2019 after being in so many different businesses; I found the one for me, Paparazzi Accessories Jewelry.

3} Being an Author and writing my own book in November 2021.

4} My husband, Darwin Sullivan and I being the Assistant Pastors of Greater St. John, December 2020 under the leadership of Bishop Russell Schaller.

5} Sunday School Superintendent of Greater St. John, December 2020.

6}Received our license and ordination papers on July 2021 from Clinton Street Greater Bethlehem Temple.

These promises 1-6 came to past by waiting on God. However, I am still waiting on some more promises to come to past.

In conclusion, when waiting on God you have to stay focused on the process. The enemy brings fear and doubt by telling you that you are too old to do the things that God is requiring of you. Remember you are never too old to fulfill God's purpose in your life. You must fight the good fight of faith and always know as long as you are living; if God said it, it is a done deal!

Matthew 24:35

Heaven and earth shall pass away, but my words shall not pass away.

SINNER'S PRAYER

The bible declares according to Romans 10:9-10 that if thou shalt confess with thy mouth the Lord Jesus, and shalt believe in thine heart that God hath raised him from the dead, thou shalt be saved. For the scripture saith, Whosoever believeth on him shall not be ashamed. Father in the Name of Jesus, I believe You are Lord. I ask You to forgive me of my sins and I shall follow Your statues all the days of my life, in Jesus' Name. Amen!

CONTACT PAGE

Pastor Rebecca Sullivan is an anointed teacher. In "Walking In God's Purpose", she shares her heartfelt testimony of how she waited on the Lord and He answered her prayers. Pastor Rebecca Sullivan is available for teaching, counseling, prayer, speaking engagements, conferences, and workshops. She can be reached at (313) 680-0297.

www.ingramcontent.com/pod-product-compliance
Lightning Source LLC
Chambersburg PA
CBHW031638160426
43196CB00006B/470